Young Golfers, Big Lessons

Life Skills Learned on the Golf Course

Illustrations and Stories by:

Kristin Sunderhaft

LPGA Teaching Professional
Life Time Member

Copyright © 2024 by Kristin Sunderhaft
All rights reserved.

All rights reserved. No part of this publication may be reproduced, distributed, or transmitted in any form or by any means, including photocopying, recording, or other electronic or mechanical methods, without the prior written permission of the publisher, except for brief quotations embodied in critical reviews and certain other noncommercial uses permitted by copyright law.

This publication is protected under the US Copyright Act of 1976 and all other applicable international, federal, state, and local laws. Any unauthorized reprint or use of this material is prohibited. No part of this book may be reproduced or transmitted by any means, electronic or mechanical, including photocopying and recording, or by any information storage or retrieval system without express written permission from the author or publisher.

DISCLAIMER

The stories and advice in **"Young Golfers, Big Lessons: Life Skills Learned on the Golf Course"** are intended for educational and inspirational purposes. While the experiences and lessons shared are inspired by real-life coaching and playing, the names and characters are fictionalized and do not necessarily represent actual persons.

Readers are encouraged to seek appropriate guidance and supervision when practicing golf or any other activities mentioned in this book. The author and publisher are not liable for any injury or damage resulting from the application of the content in this book.

Introduction and Dedication

Welcome to "Young Golfers, Big Lessons: Life Skills Learned on the Golf Course." I'm Kristin, an LPGA teaching professional with over thirty years of experience and a passion for teaching and coaching kids. This book shares golf and life lessons through the eyes of individual junior golf characters, each sharing moments on the golf course where they have learned valuable life lessons that extend beyond the course.

To all the young golfers stepping onto the fairways—this book is for you. Let these stories inspire you to embrace the values of golf and apply them in your daily life. Whether you want to learn a new sport to play with friends and family, dream of playing on your school's golf team, earn a college scholarship, or turn professional, remember that the life lessons you learn through golf are not just for now but for a lifetime, guiding you both on and off the course. May these stories of honesty, perseverance, patience, and integrity inspire you to play with determination, strive for your best, and treat others with kindness.

Golf is more than a game; it's a journey of learning and discovery that teaches valuable skills like responsibility, confidence, gratitude, and sportsmanship. These stories, drawn from real experiences, aim to enrich and guide not just young golfers but also those supporting them. They are reminders of these essential life values that we can all learn from, regardless of age or role in the game.

I want to express my heartfelt gratitude to the parents and families I've worked with over the years. Your unwavering support and encouragement have been instrumental in shaping your young golfers into the remarkable individuals they are today. This book is a testament to your dedication and belief in their potential, and I hope it continues to inspire and guide them on their journey.

I dedicate this book to my dad, who first introduced me to the game of golf. Your love, guidance, and support have shaped my journey and inspired me to follow my passion. Thank you for planting the seeds that grew into a lifelong love for golf and a career dedicated to teaching and coaching others.

Bryant's Lesson on Honesty

"Hi, I'm Bryant. Playing golf has taught me the importance of HONESTY. Playing fair and keeping the correct score is more important than just winning. It feels like a real win when I know I've been honest.

If I hit someone else's golf ball during a round, I call a penalty on myself, even if no one else noticed. Being honest on the course helps me build trust with my fellow players and enjoy the game more.

Honesty isn't just important in golf. If I find a lost wallet at school, I turn it in to the office instead of keeping it. If I accidentally break something at home, I immediately tell my parents and offer to help fix it. Being truthful helps me earn respect and build strong relationships on the golf course and in life."

Can you think of a time when you were honest, even when it was hard?

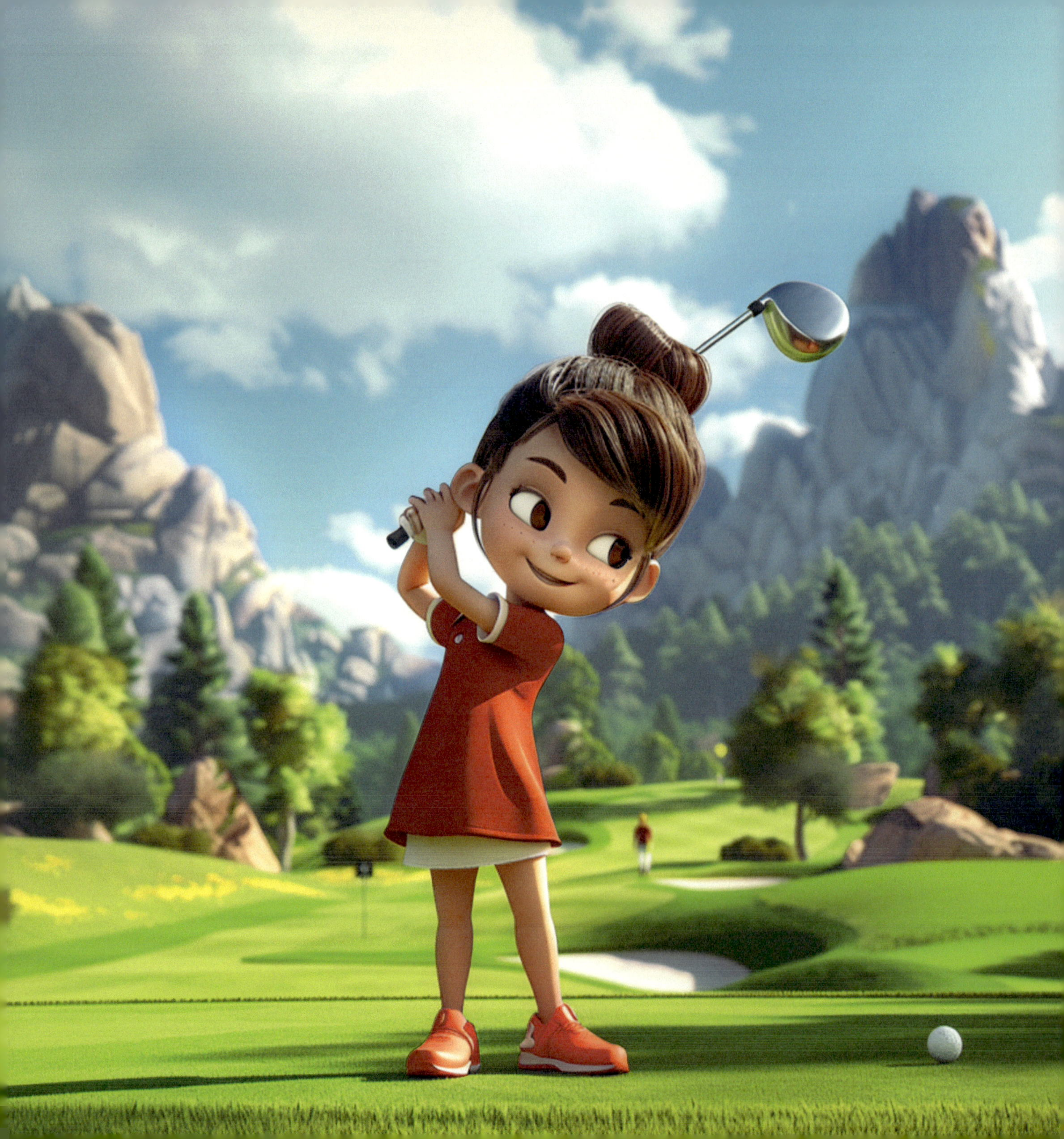

Leia's Lesson on Focus

"Hi, I'm Leia. Playing golf has taught me the importance of FOCUS. Staying focused helps me to aim my next shot and play my best. It's about concentrating and blocking out distractions.

When I'm about to swing, I take a deep breath and ignore distractions like the beverage cart or someone talking. Zeroing in on the target helps me get laser-focused so I can play better and enjoy the game more.

Focus isn't just important in golf. I listen carefully to my teacher and avoid getting distracted during class. Concentrating on what's important helps me understand the material and improve my tests and assignments. Focus helps me succeed, both on the golf course and in the classroom."

How do you avoid distractions when doing your homework?

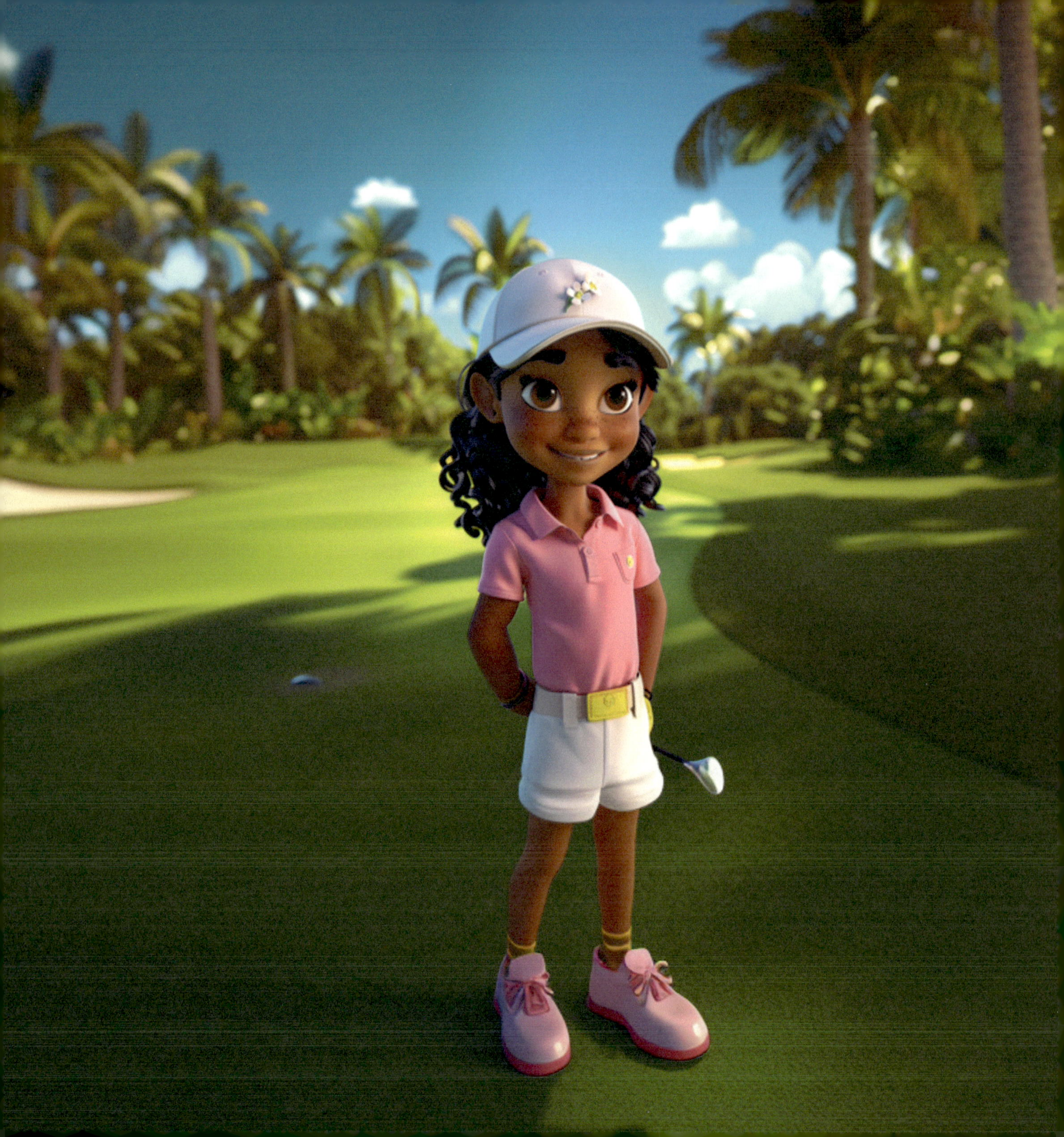

Mackenzie's Lesson on Judgment

"Hi, I'm Mackenzie. Playing golf has taught me about JUDGMENT. I learned to make smart decisions, like choosing the right club or deciding when to play it safe. This skill helps me in other areas of life, too.

Before I swing, I think about the distance to the hole, the wind, and any obstacles. Then, I choose the best club for the shot. Using good judgment on the course helps me play better and enjoy the game more.

Judgment isn't just important in golf. After school, I want to play video games, but I know I have homework. I use good judgment to finish my homework first, then reward myself with playtime. Making smart decisions helps me balance responsibilities and fun on the golf course and in life."

What helps you choose the right friends to spend time with?

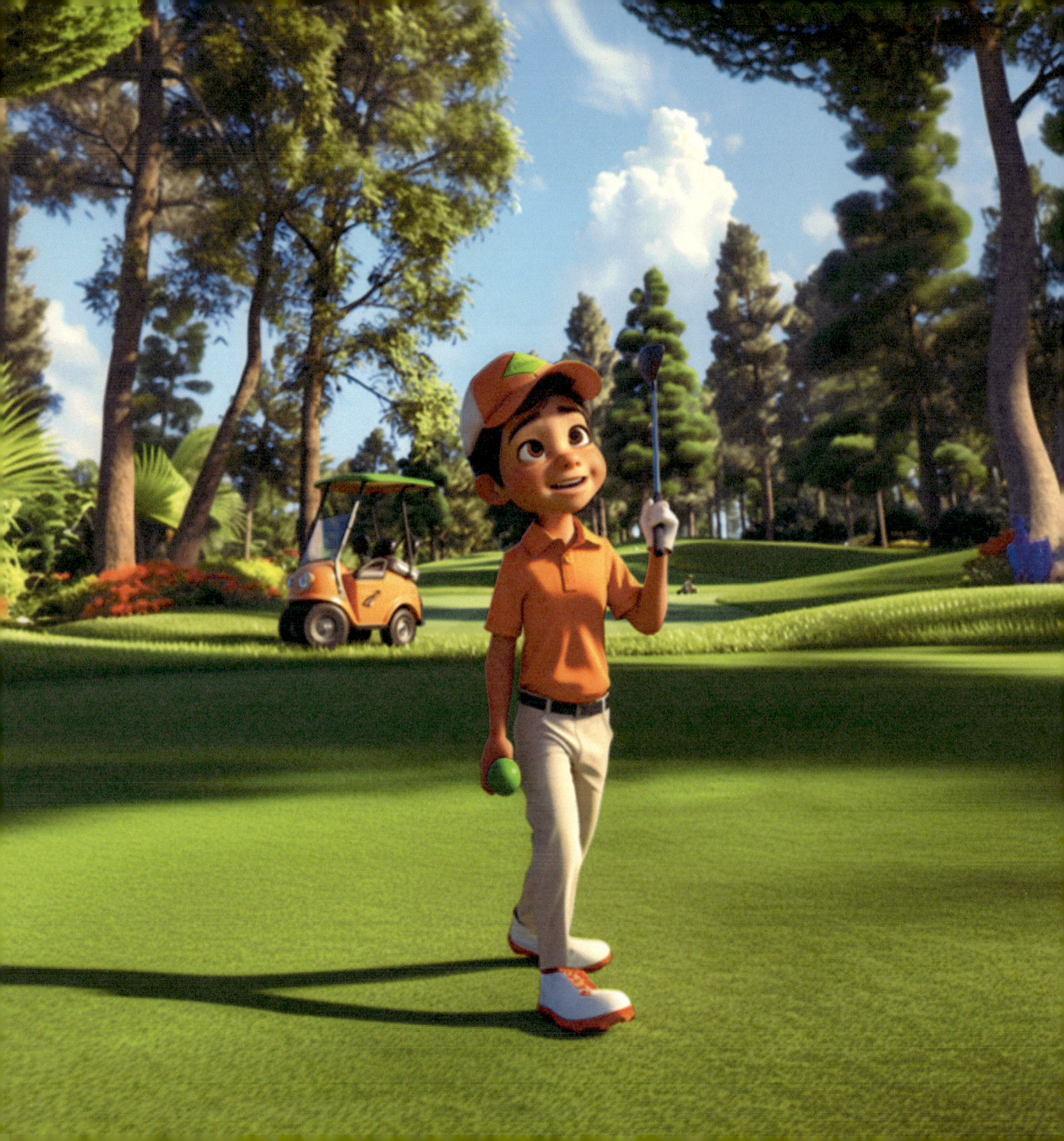

Jared's Lesson on Healthy Habits

"Hi, I'm Jared. Playing golf has taught me the importance of HEALTHY HABITS to keep my energy up and help my body perform well. This includes eating healthy, nutritious foods, getting a good night's sleep, and drinking lots of water.

Before I play, practice, or take a lesson, I always eat something healthy and drink plenty of water. I even pack healthy snacks like beef jerky, apples, hard-boiled eggs, and nuts. Those snacks help me, so find what works best for you. If I don't eat well, I know I won't play well and will lose my energy, focus, and swing. Just like my dad wouldn't put bad gas in the car, I shouldn't put bad food in my body. Our car would break down, and so would my body.

Healthy habits aren't just for golf. I start my day with a nutritious breakfast before school to stay focused and energized. A balanced dinner with fruits, vegetables, and proteins helps my body stay strong. Drinking plenty of water throughout the day keeps me hydrated and alert. A good night's sleep helps me recharge for the next day. I can do my best in golf and school by caring for my body with good food, hydration, and rest."

What are some healthy foods you can eat to give you energy for your activities?

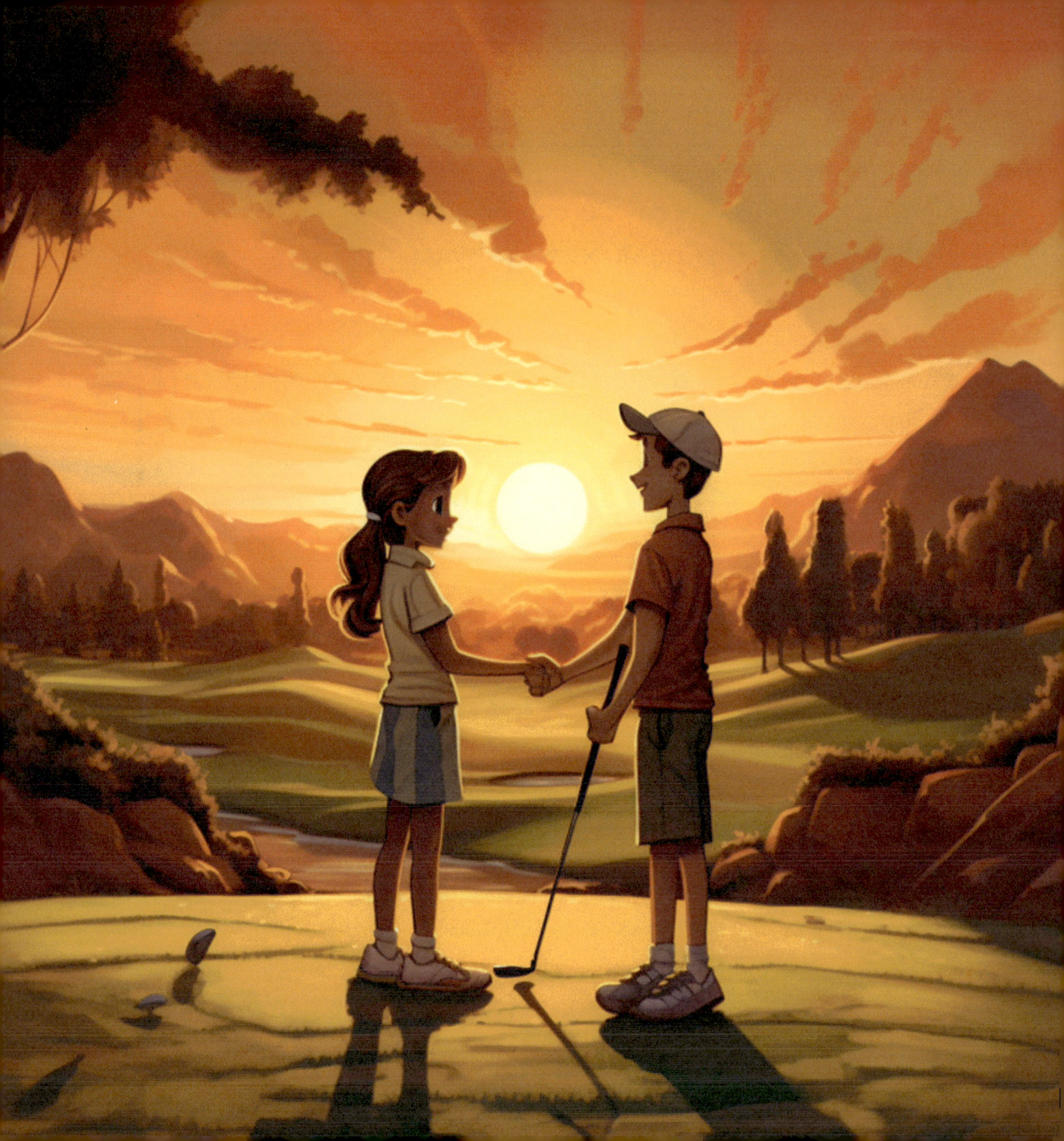

Benny's Lesson on Sportsmanship

"Hi, I'm Benny. Playing golf has taught me true SPORTSMANSHIP. Before a round, I introduce myself to new players, shaking hands and making eye contact. It's important to show courtesy and respect from the start.

When playing golf with my friends, I always cheer them on and say, 'Great Shot!' whenever they hit the ball well. Encouraging my friends makes the game more fun for everyone. If someone in our group is having a tough day, I offer encouragement to keep the mood upbeat. Being a good sport means showing respect and support, no matter how the game turns out.

Sportsmanship isn't just important in golf. At school, I congratulate my classmates when they do well on a test or in a game. Encouraging others helps build a positive environment. I also help struggling classmates by sharing study tips or offering to practice together. Whether on the golf course or in the classroom, showing sportsmanship means respecting and uplifting those around you."

How can you show good sportsmanship on and off the course?

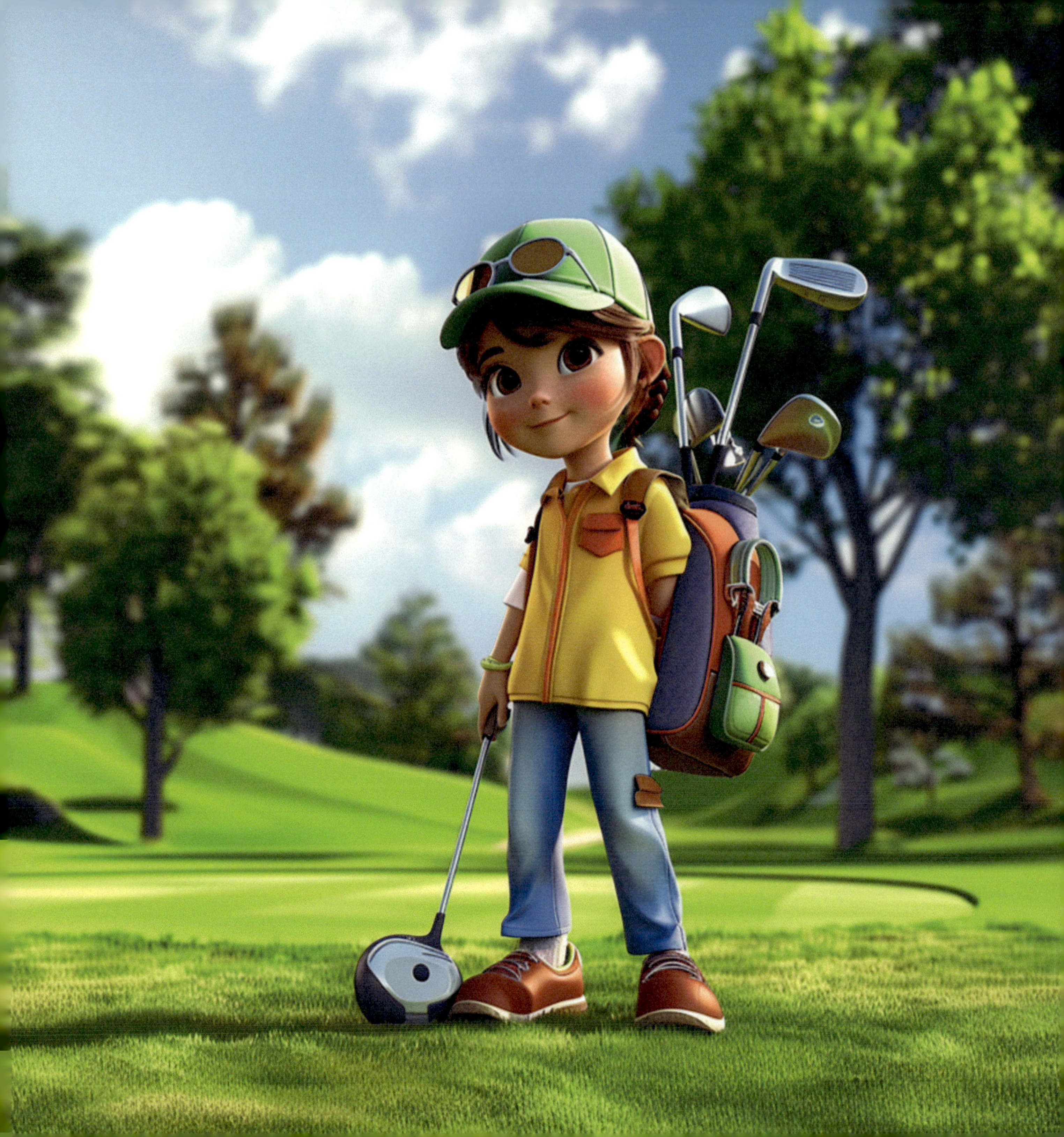

Layla's Lesson on Responsibility

"Hi, I'm Layla. Playing golf has taught me a lot about RESPONSIBILITY. After practice, I always clean my clubs and put them back in my bag. Taking care of my equipment helps me to stay organized and be ready for my next practice session or round of golf.

Before heading to the course, I make sure my golf bag has all the necessary equipment, including enough golf balls, tees, ball markers, snacks, and gloves. Being responsible means planning and being prepared. I also make sure to get to my tee time or team practice on time, showing responsibility and respect for others.

Responsibility isn't just important in golf. I do my homework right after school to stay on top of my studies. I also make sure my backpack is ready for the next day so I remember everything I need. Another example is when I say I'll be somewhere, I show up, and I'm on time. Whether on the golf course or in everyday life, taking responsibility helps me reach my goals and be relied on by others."

What are some ways you can be more responsible at home and school?

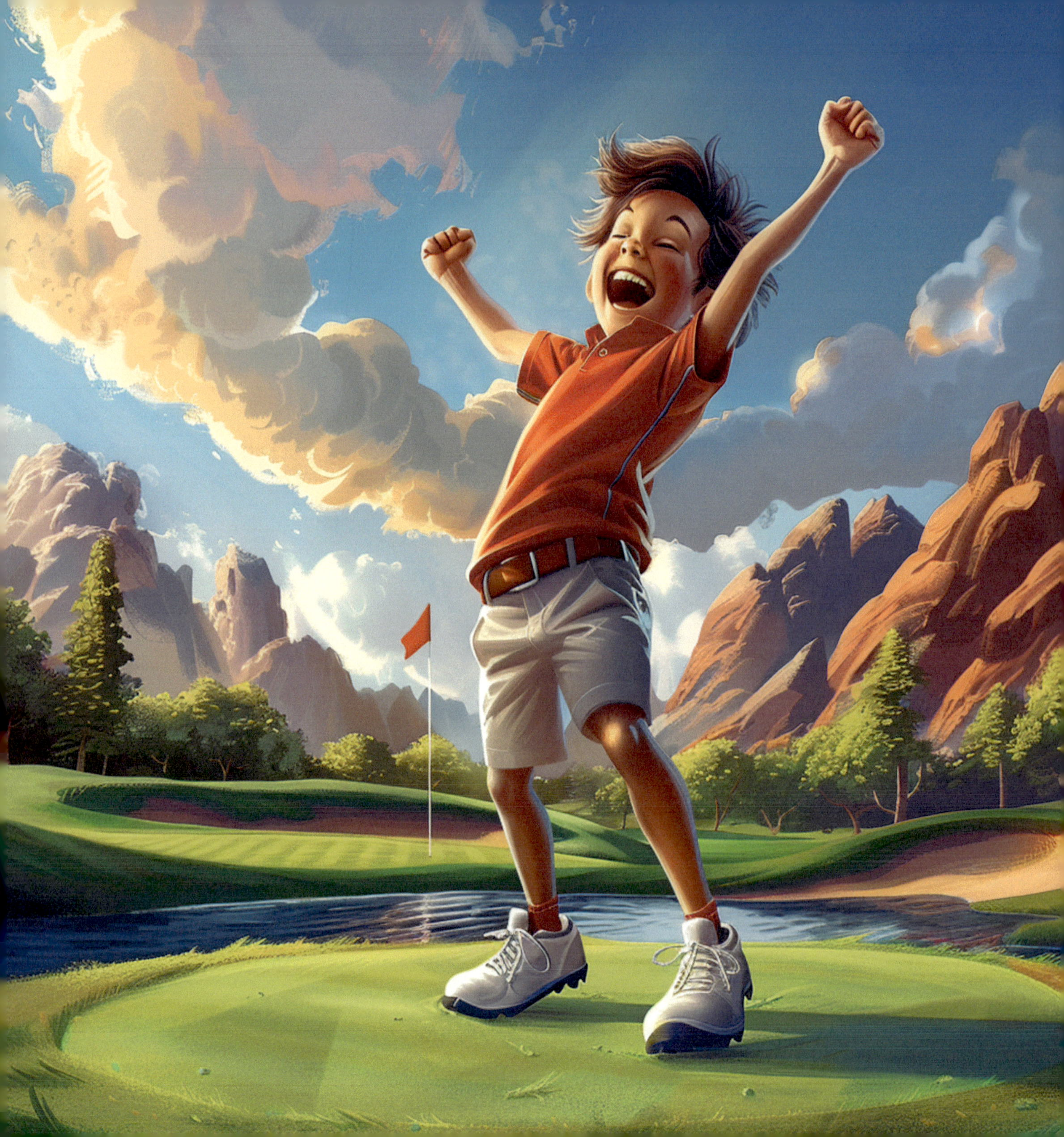

Bronson's Lesson on Confidence

"Hi, I'm Bronson. Playing golf has taught me about CONFIDENCE. Each good shot shows me that with practice, I can get better at anything. This confidence isn't just for golf; it helps me try new things in school and make new friends. Learning to believe in myself is the best lesson from golf.

When I'm about to swing, I stand tall, take a deep breath, and believe I can hit the ball well. Confidence helps me play my best and enjoy the game more. Even if I miss a shot, I remind myself that I'll keep improving with practice. Each successful swing boosts my confidence further.

Confidence isn't just important in golf. When I need to answer a question in class, I speak up and share my thoughts. Confidence helps me share my ideas and participate actively. When learning a new skill or hobby, I remind myself that I can succeed with practice and determination. Whether on the golf course or in the classroom, believing in myself allows me to grow and try new things."

Can you think of a time when you felt proud of yourself?

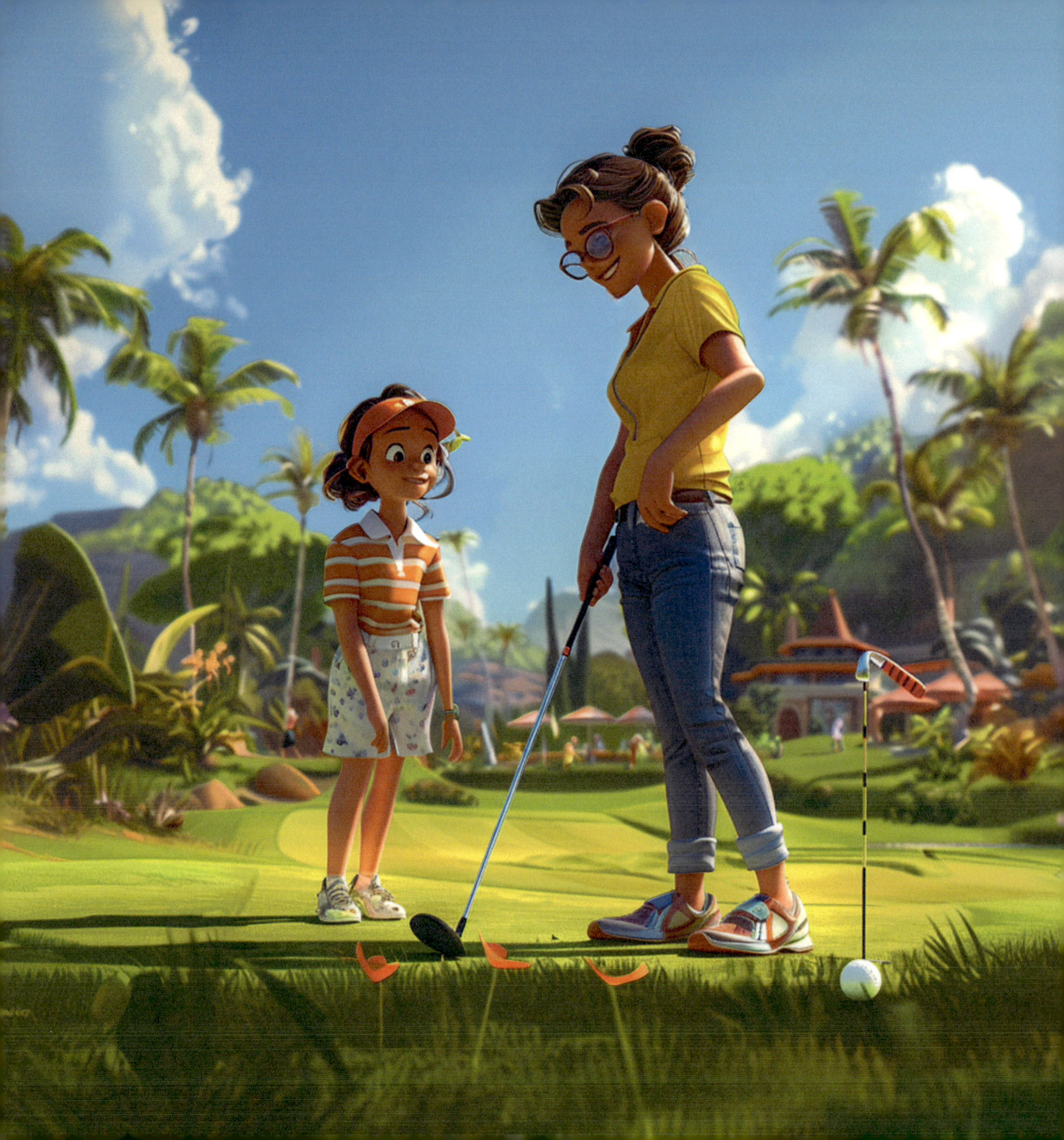

Emma's Lesson on Respect

"Hi, I'm Emma. Playing golf has taught me the importance of RESPECT. My coach shows me more than just how to swing a club; she teaches me to listen and learn from those who know more.

When my friends are taking their golf swing, I stay quiet so they can focus. Respect means letting others have their turn without distractions. Showing respect to others on the course helps everyone play their best and enjoy the game. I also show respect for the golf course by repairing any ball marks and divots and even picking up trash.

Respect isn't just important in golf. When someone is talking, I listen carefully and don't interrupt. Respect means paying attention to others. I also follow classroom rules and am polite to my teachers and classmates. Whether on the golf course or in everyday life, showing respect helps build strong and positive relationships, making interactions more enjoyable and meaningful."

How can you show respect to your friends, teachers, and family?

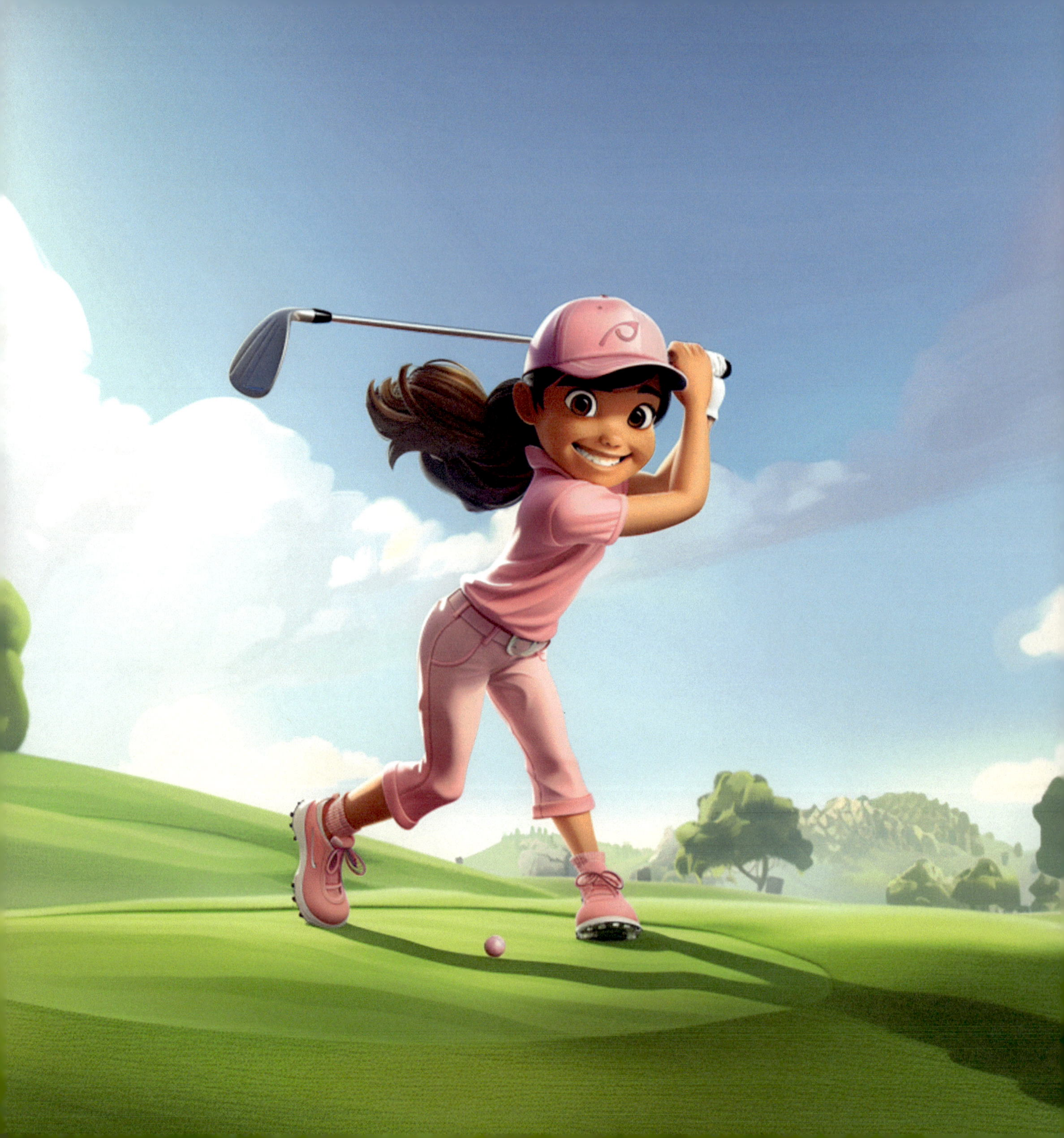

Ellie's Lesson on Integrity

"Hi, I'm Ellie. Playing golf has taught me the importance of INTEGRITY. I always count every stroke, honestly, even when no one else is watching and I miss the ball. It's embarrassing, but it teaches me to be truthful in everything I do.

Even if I have a bad round, I always write down my score. Integrity means being honest, even when changing the numbers is tempting. Staying truthful on the course helps me build trust and respect.

Integrity isn't just important in golf. I study for my tests and do my homework on my own, without copying from others. Integrity means being truthful in my schoolwork, even when taking shortcuts is easier. If I see someone drop their lunch money, I make sure to return it to them instead of keeping it. I also speak up if I see someone being treated unfairly, even if it's hard. Whether on the golf course or in everyday life, being honest and staying true to my values helps me succeed and earn the respect of others."

Why is it important to be honest, even when no one is watching?

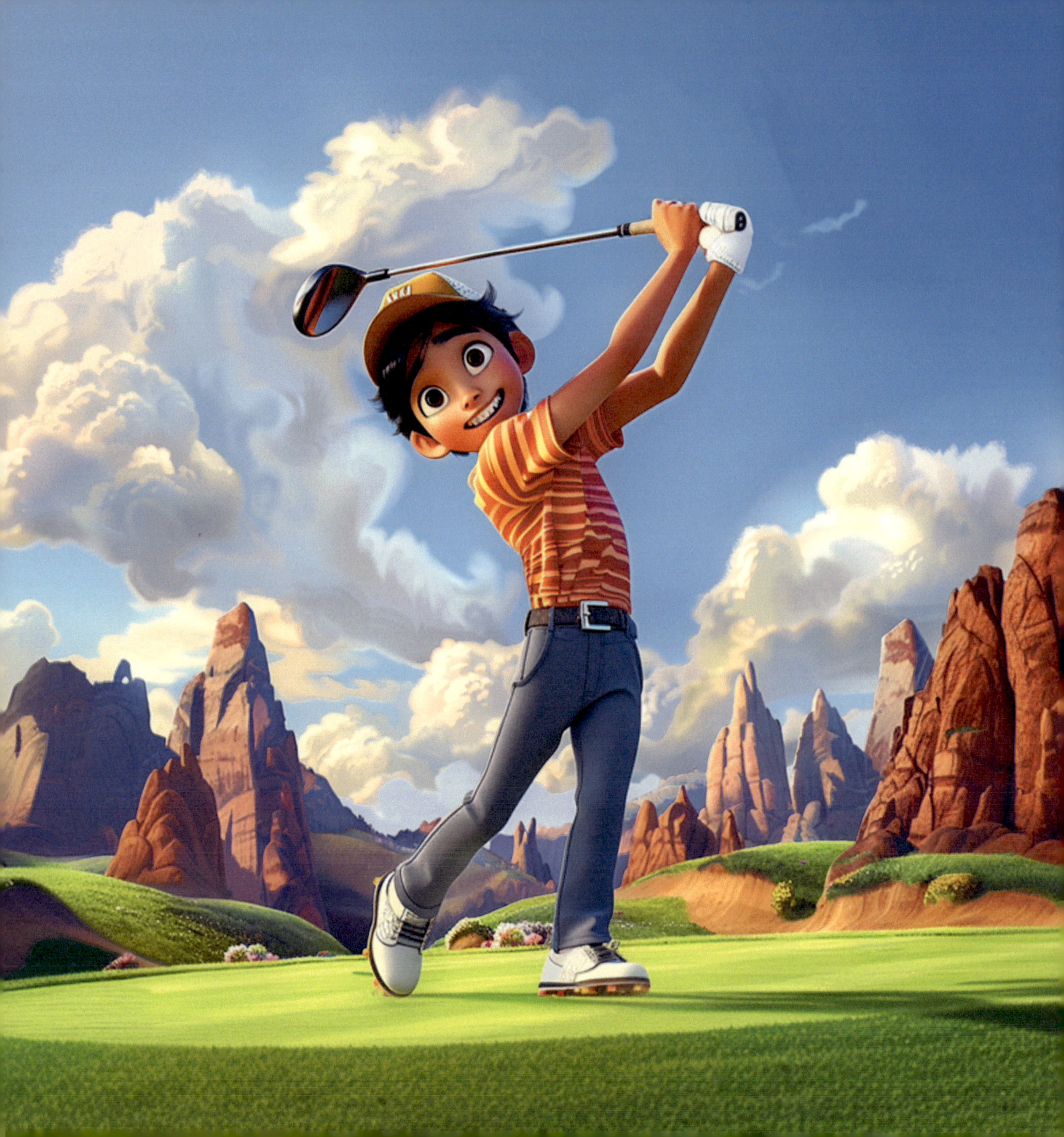

Luke's Lesson on Courtesy

"Hi, I'm Luke. Playing golf has taught me about COURTESY. On the golf course, I always remember to be polite, like being quiet when others are taking their swing and saying 'Thank You' when someone tells me I had a nice shot. Demonstrating courtesy means showing respect and kindness. Being polite on the course helps me remember to be thoughtful and considerate everywhere else, too!

If my group is playing slowly, we speed up and keep up with the group in front of us. Courtesy means considering others' time and not being a slow golfer. Being mindful of the pace of play helps everyone enjoy their game.

Courtesy isn't just important in golf. I open and hold the door for others when entering a building. And if I see an older adult who needs a seat, I give them mine. I'm young, I can stand! Courtesy means being polite and helping others. Whether on the golf course or in everyday situations, showing courtesy makes the world better for everyone."

How can you show kindness and courtesy to those around you?

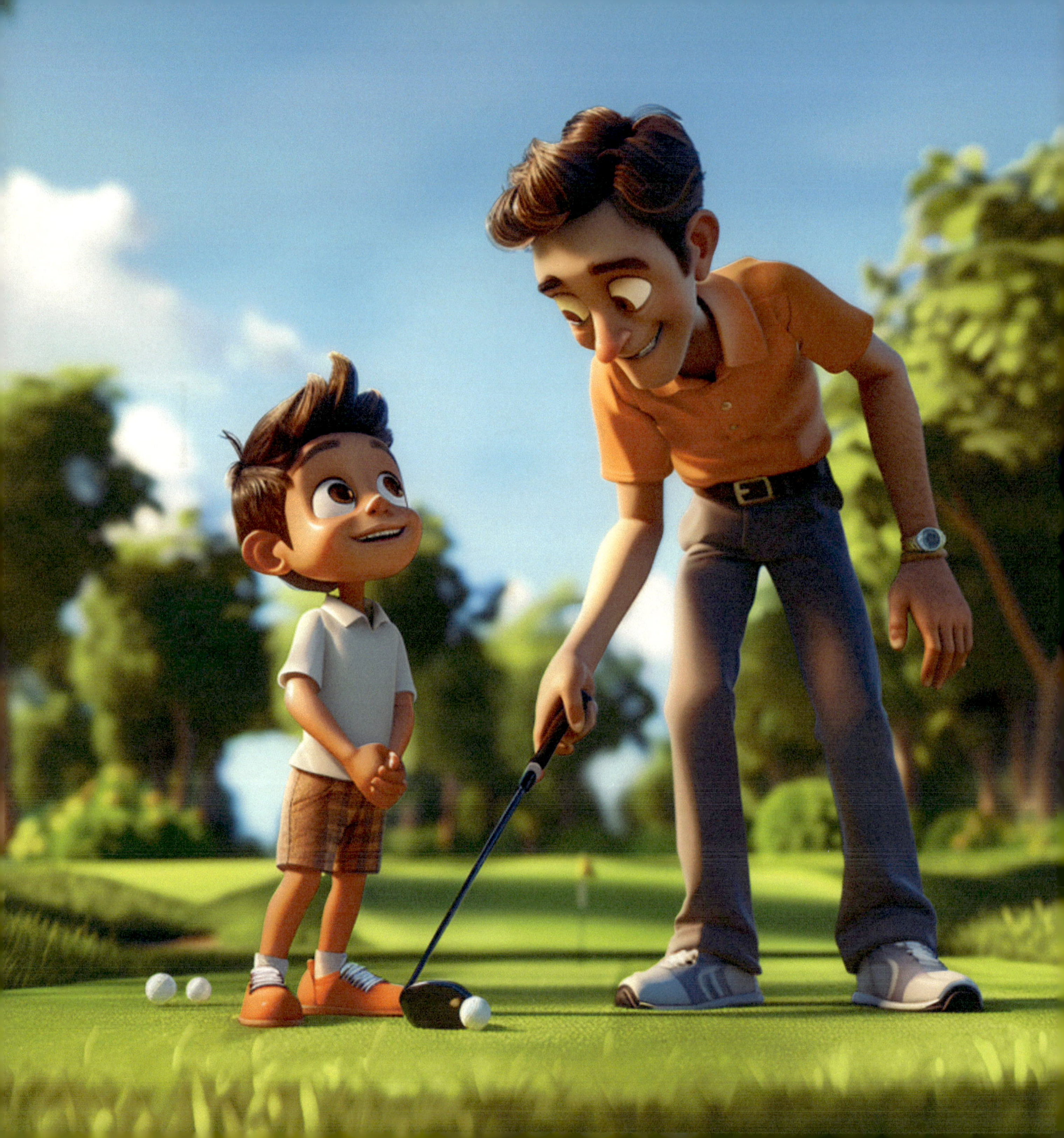

Isaac's Lesson on Enjoying the Moment

"Hi, I'm Isaac. Playing golf with my dad has taught me to ENJOY THE MOMENT and make lasting memories. It's about appreciating each other's company, learning together, and strengthening our bond.

When my dad and I play golf, we laugh, compete, and cheer each other on. Sharing these moments makes us closer and helps me appreciate our time together. Whether celebrating a great shot or encouraging each other after a miss, these experiences bring us joy and create special memories on the course.

Enjoying the moment isn't just important in golf. Spending time with my dad doing other activities, like cooking or playing games, also helps us connect and create special memories. We talk, share stories, and enjoy each other's company, strengthening our relationship. Golf has shown me how important it is to enjoy every moment and make memories that last a lifetime. Whether on the golf course or everyday life, cherishing these moments helps me build strong and meaningful relationships."

How do you make the most of the time you spend with family and friends?

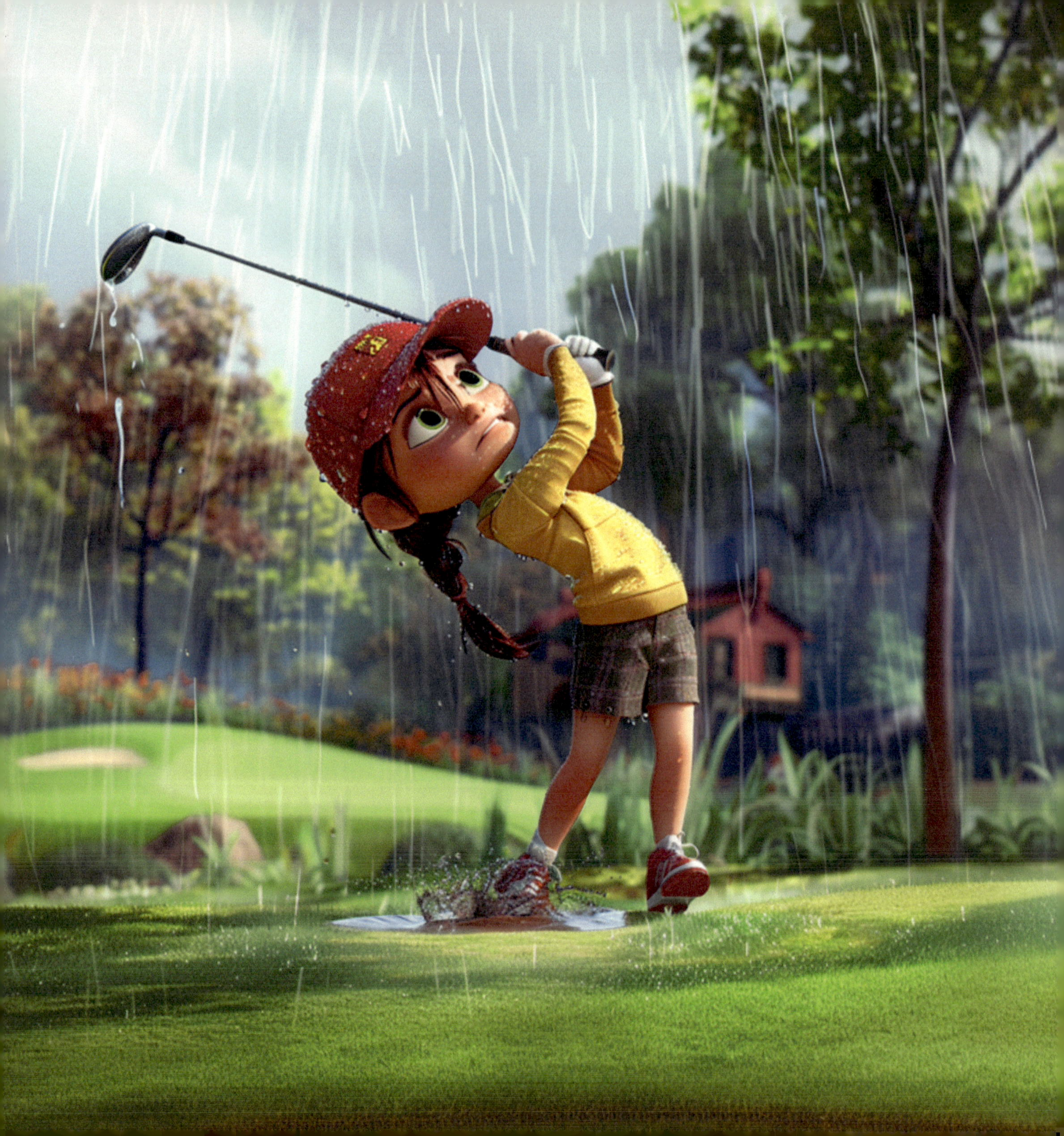

Brooklynn's Lesson on Being Adaptable

"Hi, I'm Brooklynn. Playing golf has taught me the importance of being ADAPTABLE. I've learned to adjust my approach whether the course conditions change or the weather shifts. This flexibility helps me play better no matter what. Being adaptable on the golf course has also helped me handle unexpected changes in everyday life with a positive attitude.

When it suddenly rains during a round, I quickly adapt my playing style to handle the wet conditions. Being adaptable on the golf course means staying ready for anything. If the wind picks up, I adjust my swing and aim to ensure I hit the ball where I want it to go. These experiences teach me to be flexible.

Adaptability isn't just important in golf. When unexpected changes happen, like a sudden change in plans at school or home, I use what I've learned on the golf course to stay calm and find new solutions. Whether adjusting to a new teacher or dealing with a schedule change, being adaptable helps me handle surprises easily. This ability to adapt allows me to succeed and prepares me for whatever comes next. Embracing change and staying flexible makes life's challenges more manageable and helps me grow stronger."

How do you handle unexpected changes or challenges?

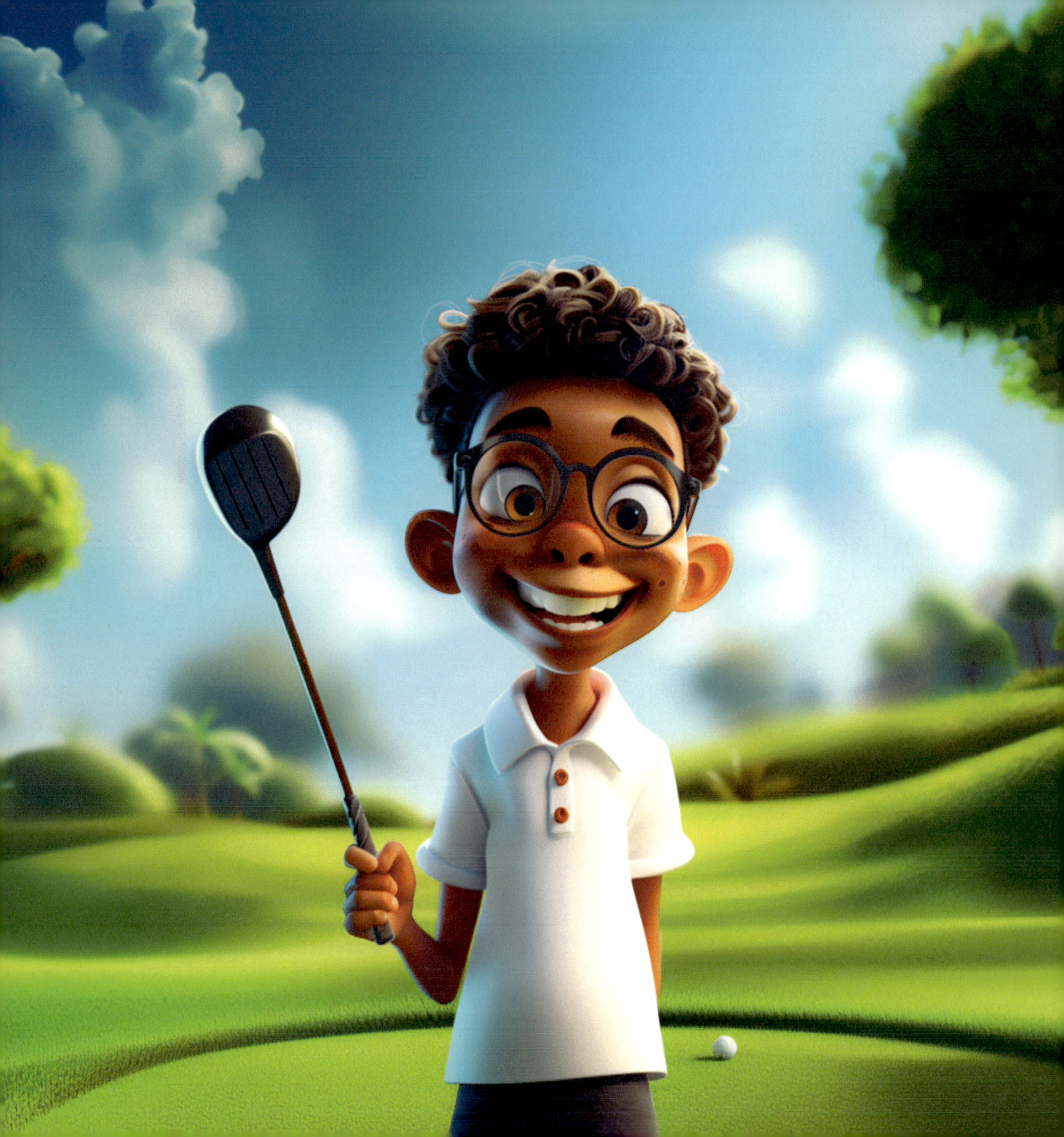

Kai's Lesson on Having a Good Attitude

"Hi, I'm Kai. Playing golf has taught me to stay POSITIVE with a GOOD ATTITUDE. Even when my shot doesn't go as planned, I focus on what I can learn from it. This helps me to keep my chin up, smile, and try again, showing that staying cheerful can improve any situation, on the course and in life!

Even if I hit a bad shot, I smile and focus on the next one. A good attitude means staying positive and not getting discouraged. It helps me enjoy the game and keeps me motivated to improve. When I miss a putt, I take a deep breath, reset, and concentrate on the next shot. If the weather changes and it starts to rain, I remind myself to have fun and embrace the challenge. Staying positive through these moments makes the game more enjoyable and helps me perform better.

Staying positive isn't just important in golf. If I get a low grade on a test, I remain positive and work harder for the next one. A good attitude means believing I can improve. When I face challenges, like learning a new skill or dealing with a difficult situation, I remind myself to stay hopeful and keep trying. Whether on the golf course or in everyday life, having a good attitude helps me overcome obstacles and achieve my goals."

How can you keep a positive attitude even when things are tough?

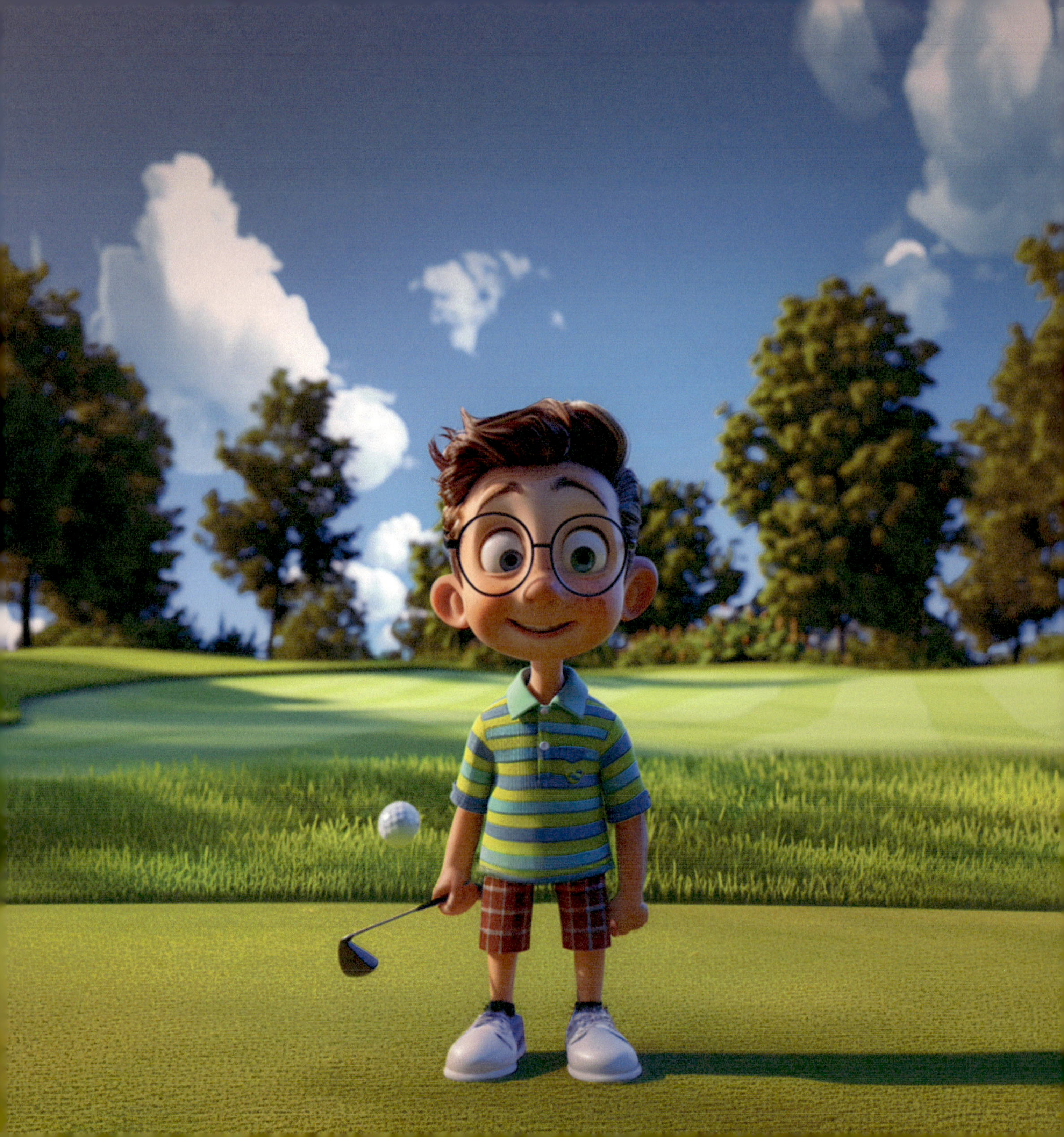

Lleyton's Lesson on Being Kind

"Hi, I'm Lleyton. Playing golf has taught me about BEING KIND. I always say 'Good Shot!' to my friends when they hit the ball well. Being kind on the golf course helps us all enjoy the game more.

If a fellow golfer loses their golf ball, I help them look for it. Being kind means going out of your way to assist others in need. Helping others shows that you care about their experience and are willing to support them.

Kindness isn't just important in golf. Writing a thank you note when someone gives me a gift shows that I appreciate their thoughtfulness. Being kind means expressing gratitude and making others feel valued. I also show kindness daily by complimenting someone or sharing my snacks. Being kind on the golf course or in everyday situations helps build a positive and supportive environment."

What are some kind things you can do for your friends and family?

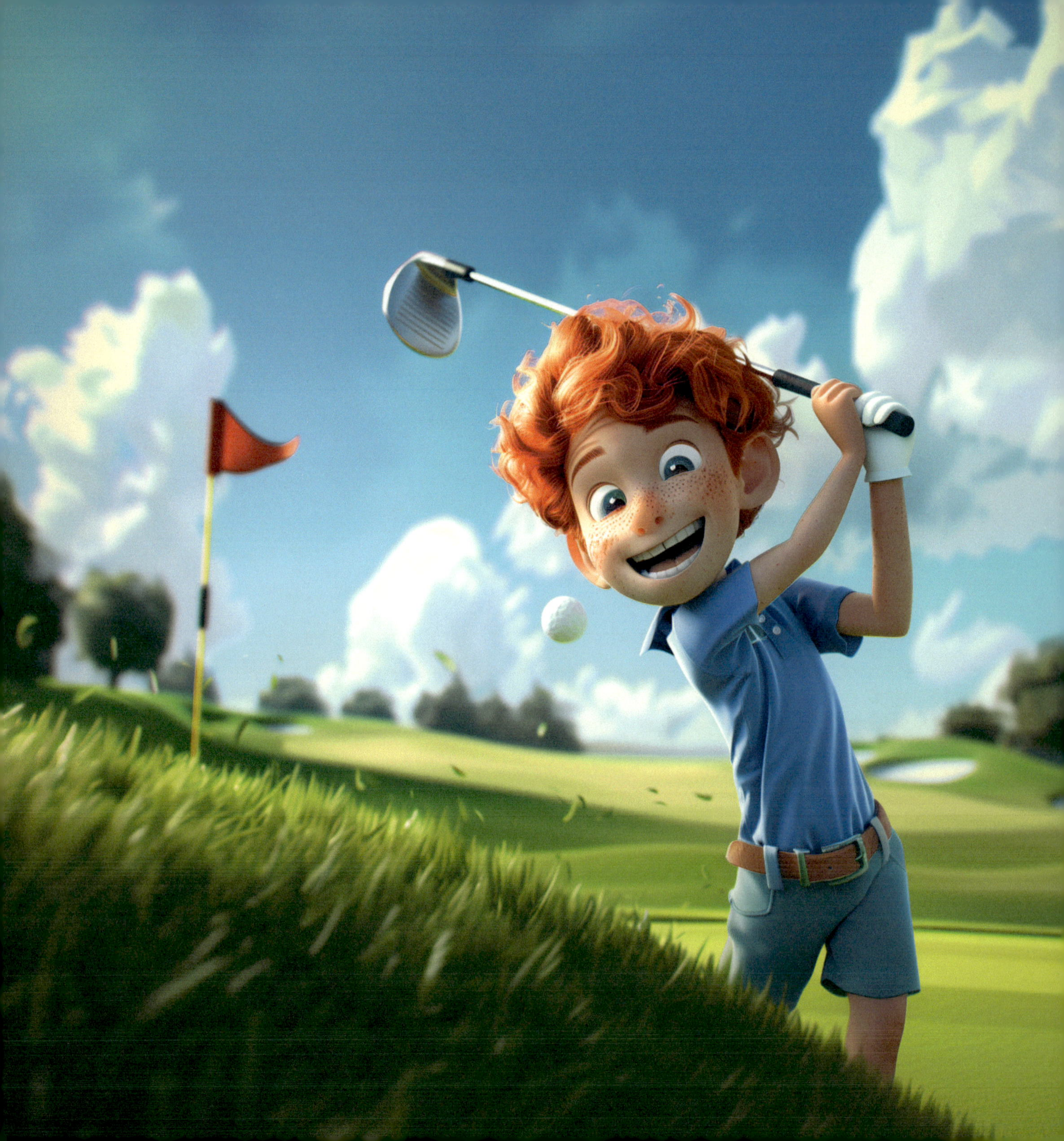

Oliver's Lesson on Perseverance

"Hi, I'm Oliver. Golf is challenging, but it teaches me to KEEP GOING and PERSEVERE even when it gets frustrating. It's a game where I've learned never to give up, helping me stick with my golf goals and with everything I do!

When I hit a bad golf shot, I don't give up. I take a deep breath, focus, and try my best on the next shot. Perseverance helps me improve and enjoy the game. Each shot is a chance to learn and get better. You never know; that next shot could be a hole-in-one! Always learn from the experience and move on.

Perseverance isn't just important in golf. When my homework is tough, I don't give up. I keep trying and ask for help if I need it. Perseverance helps me learn and do well in school. It means sticking with it until I get better, even if I need a tutor. Whether on the golf course or in the classroom, not giving up and staying determined helps me achieve my goals."

Can you think of a challenge you overcame by not giving up?

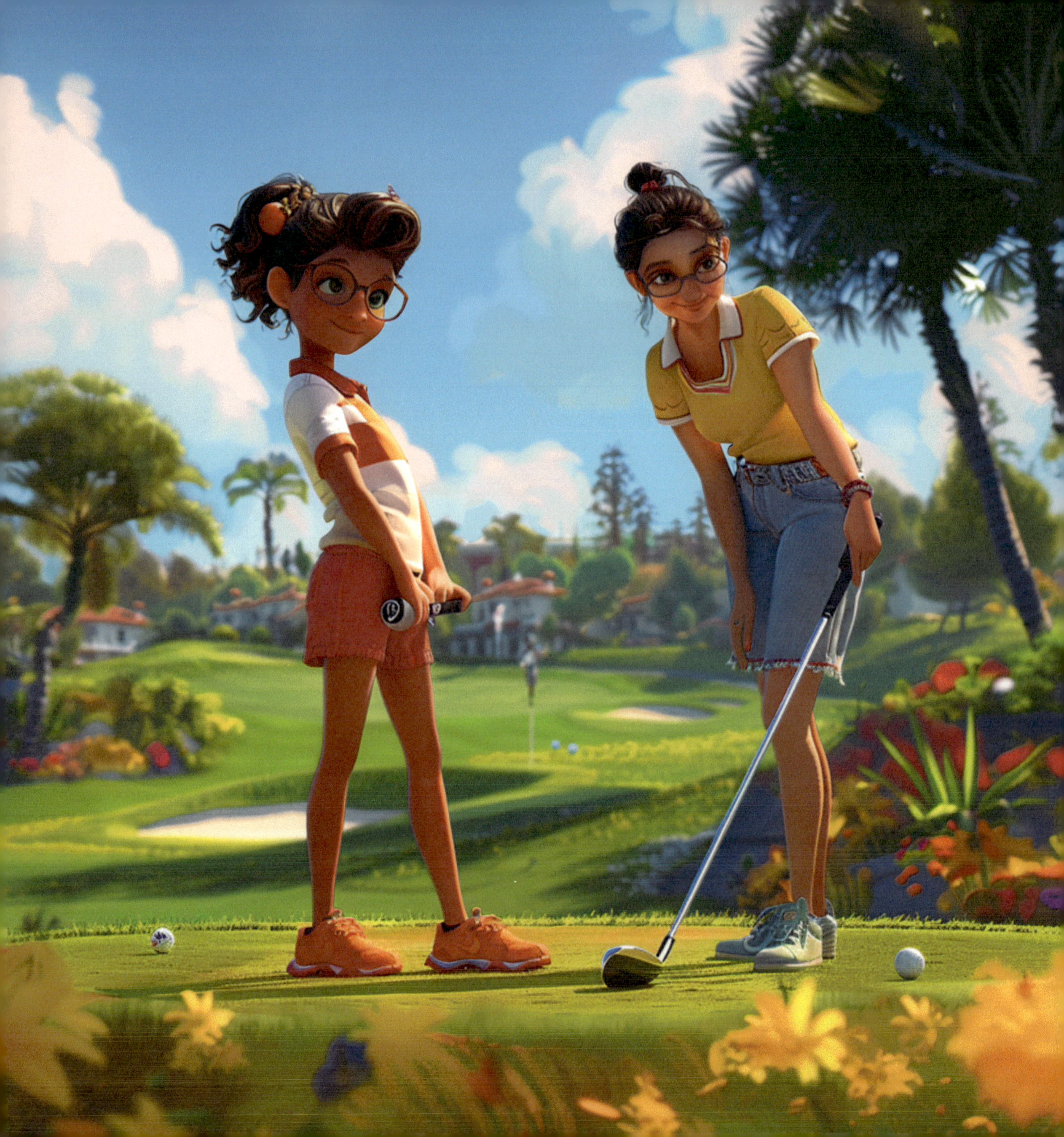

Scarlett and Brynnlee's Lesson on Gratitude

"Hi, we're Scarlett and Brynnlee. Playing golf together teaches us to be GRATEFUL for the time we spend with each other and the fun we have on the course. We always remind each other how blessed we are to play this game and share our friendship.

We express our gratitude by thanking each other for being great friends and making the game fun. Acting as accountability partners, we motivate each other to practice and play regularly, which helps us get better and enjoy the game even more.

Gratitude isn't just important in golf. We show gratitude by thanking our families for their support and appreciating the opportunities we have. Being grateful helps us stay positive and cherish the moments we spend with good friends on and off the golf course. Whether on the course or in everyday life, gratitude makes our experiences richer and more meaningful."

What are you thankful for, and how do you show your gratitude?

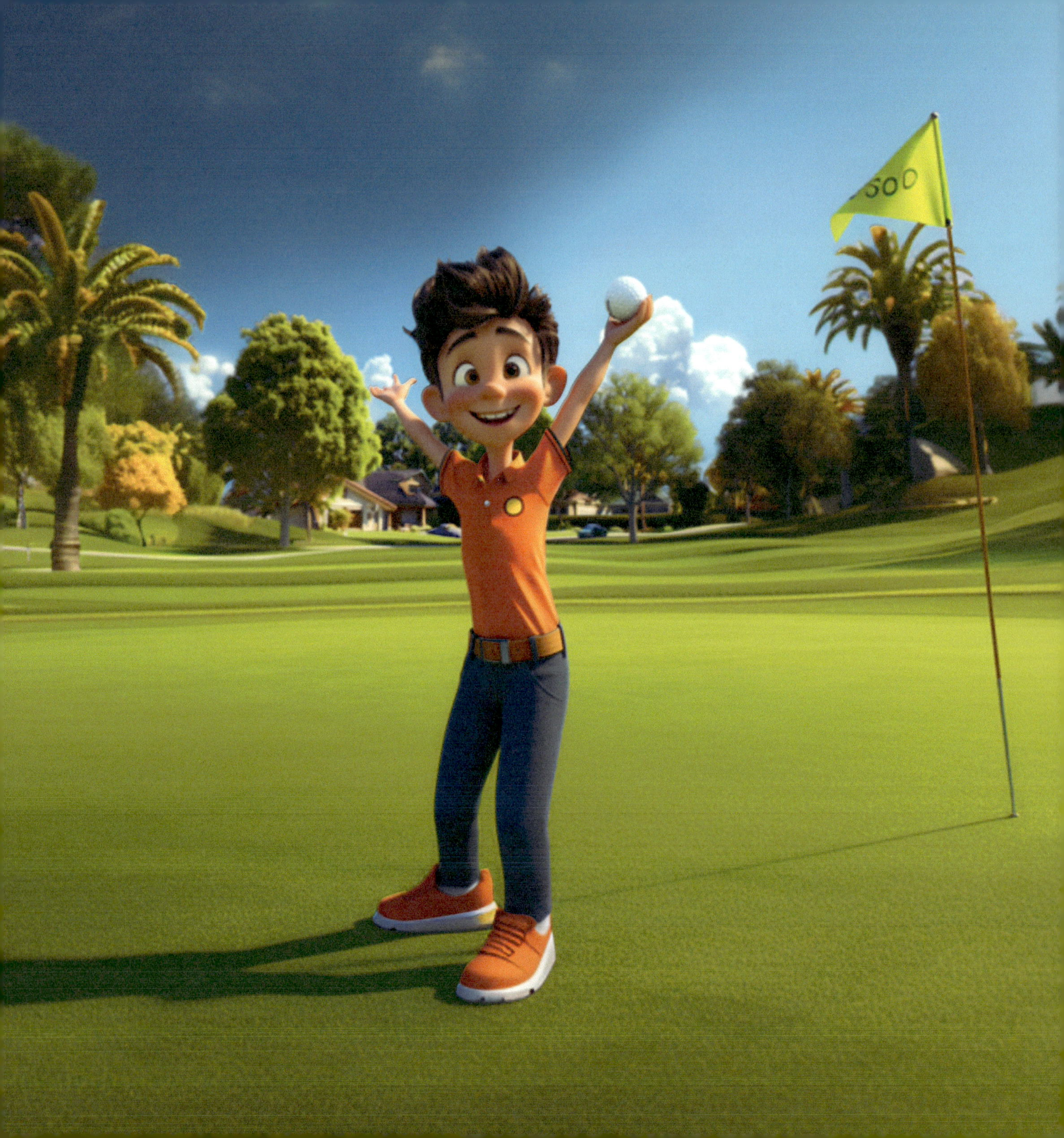

Jett's Lesson on Patience

"Hi, I'm Jett. Playing golf has taught me to be PATIENT. My golf game improves little by little, showing me that growing and getting better takes time. I've learned that it's okay for things to take time in golf and with everything I do!

I take my time on each shot in golf by doing a pre-shot routine. Patience helps me make better decisions and play better golf. When I miss a putt, I stay calm and carefully line up the next shot. I also practice regularly, understanding that each session brings me closer to my goals, no matter how small the progress. Patience means enjoying the journey and celebrating each slight improvement along the way.

Patience isn't just important in golf. When I have a challenging math problem, I take my time to think it through and try different ways to solve it. Instead of getting frustrated, I remember finding the correct answer requires time and effort. I also apply patience when learning a new skill, like playing an instrument or building a model. Patience helps me stay focused and persistent, whether on the golf course or in the classroom. By being patient, I can achieve my goals and enjoy the process of learning and growing."

How do you practice patience when things don't go as planned?

Coach Kristin's Lesson on Following Your Heart

The game of golf has taught me the importance of FOLLOWING YOUR HEART. I have experienced a fulfilling journey because I learned to follow my heart. It all started with a simple introduction to golf and playing with my dad at eight years old in Syracuse, NY. Moving to Columbus, OH, watching the Jack Nicklaus Memorial Golf Tournament in person for several years, and working on the grounds crew at Scioto CC during college summer breaks planted many seeds. Those seeds kept tapping into my heart until I finally pursued a career in golf, discovering a profound passion for working with kids.

I am thankful, grateful, honored, and blessed to have been able to do what I love for so many years and meet so many amazing people and families along the way. Teaching golf has been an extraordinary journey, and sharing these stories with you has been a dream come true.

Following your heart isn't just important in golf; it's essential in life. When you follow your passions, you open yourself up to incredible experiences and opportunities. The lessons we learn on the golf course will guide us in life, helping us grow and become the best versions of ourselves. Whether on the fairway or navigating life, always follow your heart and pursue what you love.

Thank you for joining me on this journey. May every step you take be guided by your heart and filled with purpose and passion.

Coach Kristin Sunderhaft, LPGA

What activities or hobbies bring you joy and excitement?

Made in the USA
Columbia, SC
20 March 2025